PERSPECTIVES ON AMERICAN PROGRESS

BARACK OBAMA
IS ELECTED PRESIDENT

BY DUCHESS HARRIS, JD, PHD

Cover image: Barack Obama waves to supporters after winning the 2008 election.

Core Library

An Imprint of Abdo Publishing
abdopublishing.com

abdopublishing.com

Published by Abdo Publishing, a division of ABDO, PO Box 398166, Minneapolis, Minnesota 55439. Copyright © 2019 by Abdo Consulting Group, Inc. International copyrights reserved in all countries. No part of this book may be reproduced in any form without written permission from the publisher. Core Library™ is a trademark and logo of Abdo Publishing.

Printed in the United States of America, North Mankato, Minnesota
022018
092018

Cover Photo: Morry Gash/AP Images
Interior Photos: Morry Gash/AP Images, 1; Matt Rourke/AP Images, 4–5, 43; Paul Sancya/AP Images, 7; Obama Press Office/New/Newscom, 12–13; Red Line Editorial, 17, 40; Jae C. Hong/AP Images, 18; Seth Poppel/Yearbook Library, 20–21; Ron Edmonds/AP Images, 26–27; Charles Ommanney/Getty Images News/Getty Images, 29; Charlie Neibergall/AP Images, 31; AP Images, 34–35; Jim Bourg/Reuters/Newscom, 39

Editor: Marie Pearson
Imprint Designer: Maggie Villaume
Series Design Direction: Ryan Gale
Contributor: Don Nardo

Library of Congress Control Number: 2017962647

Publisher's Cataloging-in-Publication Data

Names: Harris, Duchess, author.
Title: Barack Obama is elected president / by Duchess Harris.
Description: Minneapolis, Minnesota : Abdo Publishing, 2019. | Series: Perspectives on American progress | Includes online resources and index.
Identifiers: ISBN 9781532114878 (lib.bdg.) | ISBN 9781532154706 (ebook)
Subjects: LCSH: Obama, Barack, 1961-.--Juvenile literature. | Elections--United States--Juvenile literature. | Presidents--United States--Election--History--Juvenile literature. | African American presidential candidates--Juvenile literature.
Classification: DDC 328.73092 [B]--dc23

CONTENTS

CHAPTER ONE
Taking a Huge Risk 4

CHAPTER TWO
"Change We Can Believe In" 12

CHAPTER THREE
Politics and Family 20

CHAPTER FOUR
An Inspired Campaign Manager . . 26

CHAPTER FIVE
War Hero and Maverick Senator . . 34

Important Dates 42

Stop and Think 44

Glossary 45

Online Resources 46

Learn More 46

About the Author 47

Index 48

CHAPTER ONE

TAKING A HUGE RISK

On March 18, 2008, Barack Obama stood before spectators and cameras in Philadelphia, Pennsylvania. The media reported that he was about to deliver a controversial speech. There was also buzz in political circles. It said giving the speech would be a huge risk for Obama. He was running as the Democratic Party's candidate for president. He had a chance to be the first African-American US president. His campaign was strong. But his opponent, Arizona senator John McCain, was also campaigning hard.

Obama's March 18 speech was called "A More Perfect Union."

On March 13, ABC News had aired a shocking video. It showed clips of Obama's pastor, Reverend Jeremiah Wright. Wright was speaking at Trinity Church in Chicago, Illinois. He condemned the US government. He claimed the government was corrupt and racist.

A Look at Race Relations?

Wright's harsh words put Obama in a tough spot. The candidate had attended Trinity for 20 years. Some people agreed with Wright's comments. Obama did not. In a public statement he called them "appalling." He added, "I reject outright the statements by Rev. Wright."

It quickly became clear that this distancing was not enough. Obama saw that the controversy was starting to hurt his campaign. He decided to address the issue in a speech. Obama also wanted to talk about the wider issue of racial prejudice in the United States.

Obama distanced himself from Wright's views so they would not be mistaken as his own.

In the speech, he focused on the topic of race relations. As a people, he said, Americans had never fully dealt with the nation's racial problems. He urged his listeners to take an honest look at race relations. If they could not, the country could not become fully unified.

A Positive Trend

Obama knew that giving the speech was risky. Some people might see him as being too concerned about race. That perception might keep them from voting for him. But he felt the issue was too important to ignore.

Some people were disappointed that Obama rejected Wright's comments. They felt Wright was supporting a group that had faced a history of mistreatment. But Obama's choice to give the speech paid off. It was widely praised. That praise proved to be part of a positive trend. As the months rolled by, many national polls were taken. Obama came out ahead in most of them. This showed that more voters were leaning toward him than toward McCain. Obama held his lead into the week of the election in early November 2008.

That week still proved to be a highly dramatic one. McCain's followers insisted that he might come from behind and win. Tensions rose on election day, November 4, 2008. A major question on nearly everyone's mind was whether or not history would be made. Would Barack Obama

PERSPECTIVES
DIFFERING VIEWS

Many Americans praised Obama's speech on race. Among them was historian Garry Wills. He described its wording as very effective and moving. A number of scholars, Wills points out, went further. They felt it was one of the finest speeches ever given by an American. A few were critical of the speech, however. Some black writers felt that Rev. Wright's views were correct. Racism was deeply imbedded in American society and government. Among those critics was noted black religious scholar Obery Hendricks. He claimed the speech was politically motivated. Obama had to condemn Wright in order to maintain the support of white voters, Hendricks said.

THE ELECTORAL COLLEGE

American presidents are not chosen directly by the people. Instead, the Electoral College chooses them. It is not a school. Rather, it is a group of officials called electors. Each state has a certain number of electors based on its population. Electors usually must vote for the winner of the popular vote in each state. The most populous state, California, had 55 electors in 2008. States with the fewest people had only 3 electors each. There are 538 electors in all. To become president, a candidate has to get 270 electoral votes. That is half the total number of electors plus one.

become the first African-American US president? The answer to that question came that night. Obama won a major victory, gaining 365 electoral votes. McCain won only 173. Obama had made history. His victorious campaign was driven by many people who each brought their own perspectives to the race.

STRAIGHT TO THE
SOURCE

On March 18, 2008, Obama spoke about
race relations:

*This was one of the tasks we set forth at the beginning
of this presidential campaign: to continue the long march
of those who came before us, a march for a more just, more
equal, more free, more caring, and more prosperous America.
I chose to run for President at this moment in history because I
believe deeply that we cannot solve the challenges of our time
unless we solve them together, unless we perfect our union by
understanding that we may have different stories, but we hold
common hopes; that we may not look the same and may not
have come from the same place, but we all want to move in the
same direction: towards a better future for our children and our
grandchildren. And this belief comes from my unyielding faith in
the decency and generosity of the American people.*

Source: "Barack Obama: 'A More Perfect Union.'" *American
Rhetoric Online Speech Bank.* American Rhetoric, March 18,
2008. Web. Accessed October 3, 2017.

What's the Big Idea?
Read this excerpt from Obama's famous race relations
speech carefully. What is the main idea of the
passage? Name two or three pieces of evidence
in the passage that support this idea.

CHAPTER
TWO

"CHANGE WE CAN BELIEVE IN"

Barack Obama was born on August 4, 1961, in Honolulu. It is the largest city on the Hawaiian island of Oahu. None of Obama's relatives were from Hawaii. His mother, Ann Dunham, was born in Kansas. His father, Barack Hussein Obama Sr., was from Kenya, Africa. The two met while attending the University of Hawaii.

Their son, Barack Jr., and his mother lived in Indonesia when he was young. Obama moved back to Hawaii in 1971. He went to private school in Honolulu. He earned good grades and was a star on the school

Obama, *number 23*, played basketball at Punahou School in Honolulu.

basketball team. Obama graduated from high school in 1979. He attended college in Los Angeles, California, for two years. While there, he gained an interest in politics. Obama heard that New York City's Columbia University had a good political science program. So he went there next. He graduated in 1983 at age 22.

Preparing to Be a Leader

Obama now seriously considered entering politics. But he was still very young and lacked experience. He saw he must learn how to work with the public. So he became a community organizer. He worked in impoverished neighborhoods. He taught the residents how to improve run-down homes, schools, and parks. Everyone who met him agreed he excelled at the job.

Obama felt he could do more. He decided a better knowledge of the law would help. In 1988 he began studying law at Harvard University in Cambridge, Massachusetts. He graduated with high honors in 1991. The following year, he married a young lawyer named Michelle Robinson.

A Professional Politician

With his wife's blessing, Obama finally began his political career in 1996. Then 35, he ran for Illinois state senate. He won and served as senator until 2004. That year he ran for the US Senate and won. As a senator in Washington, DC, Obama sponsored many legislative bills. He also worked closely with several Republicans.

Still Obama was not satisfied with his success. He felt he could help even more Americans if he

LOSING A CAMPAIGN

Obama ran for an Illinois seat in the US House of Representatives in 2000. His opponent was Bobby Rush. Rush had held the seat for eight years. He was known for his work during the civil rights movement. This movement promoted equal treatment of African Americans. At that time, Rush was part of the Black Panther Party. It protected black people from violence. Rush helped arrange Black Panther meal programs for children in poverty. Obama lost the campaign. But more people began recognizing his name.

PERSPECTIVES
POSSIBLE ONLY IN AMERICA

In July 2004, Obama gained national attention. He gave a major speech at the Democratic Party's national convention. His speech followed the campaign's theme of change. He celebrated Americans' belief that small yet important changes can be made. He saw a need for change in areas such as health care and job security, and he wanted to be the one to bring that change.

were president. He announced his entry into the 2008 presidential race on February 10, 2007. In an inspiring speech, he said the country was great. But it could be even greater. He wanted to change the nation.

A Message of Change

Obama was intent on bringing about positive change. So he made it his campaign's main theme. His slogan was "Change We Can Believe In." Part of the change he promised was to provide more people with health insurance.

MAY 2008

SPEECHES AND INTERVIEWS

This timeline shows Obama's speech and interview schedule for May 2008. He had appointments across the nation. Why do you think he had so many?

- **May 3** — Speech in Indiana
- **May 4** — Interview with NBC News
- **May 5** — Interview with CNN; Interview with CBS News
- **May 6** — Speech after the Indiana and North Carolina Primaries
- **May 8** — Interview with CNN
- **May 9** — Speech in Oregon
- **May 12** — Speech in West Virginia
- **May 13** — Speech in Missouri
- **May 14** — Speech in Michigan
- **May 18** — Speech in Oregon
- **May 20** — Speech after the Kentucky and Oregon Primaries
- **May 21** — Speech in Iowa
- **May 23** — Speech in Florida
- **May 25** — Speech in Connecticut
- **May 26** — Speech in New Mexico
- **May 27** — Speech in Nevada
- **May 28** — Exchange with Reporters

Many Americans responded well to that message. Others supported Obama because he was knowledgeable on policy issues. Still others saw him as mature and thoughtful. For these and other reasons, his popularity soared. On November 2, 2008, he expressed confidence he would win. Two days later, he did just that.

EXPLORE ONLINE

Chapter Two tells about how Barack Obama entered politics and ran for various public offices, including US president. The article at the website below goes into more depth on this topic. Does the article answer any of the questions you had about Obama's rise as a politician?

CNN: BARACK OBAMA: A METEORIC RISE
abdocorelibrary.com/barack-obama-elected

Obama and his family appeared before voters after the election to thank them for their support.

CHAPTER
THREE

POLITICS AND FAMILY

Barack Obama's wife, Michelle, was born on January 17, 1964, in Chicago, Illinois. Before she married Obama, her name was Michelle LaVaughn Robinson. Early on, she showed her intelligence. She graduated from high school in 1981. Her grades were the second highest in her class.

In her late teens, Robinson attended Princeton University, in Princeton, New Jersey. She graduated with honors in 1985. Next, she studied law at Harvard University. After graduating, she became a lawyer at a Chicago law firm. She met young Barack Obama at the firm in 1989. They married in

Michelle was student council treasurer her senior year of high school.

October 1992. In 1998 they had their first daughter, Malia. Their second daughter, Sasha, was born in 2001.

TWO YOUNG LAWYERS FALL IN LOVE

When Michelle Robinson met Barack Obama, she was a young lawyer. She worked at a Chicago law firm. In 1989, the firm hired Obama. It assigned Robinson to be his adviser. Soon the two began dating. Two years later, Obama proposed. She said yes, and they married on October 3, 1992.

In the National Spotlight

When her husband decided to run for president, Michelle no longer had time for her own career. She now worked full time on two fronts. One job was caring for young Malia and Sasha. The other was helping her husband's campaign.

Michelle now found herself in the national spotlight. She was the first African-American woman to become a potential First Lady. Michelle knew there was discrimination against black people. Some associated black people with broken families and an inability to keep steady jobs. She saw it as important to show that a black family could have healthy family bonds and be successful.

Hoping to strengthen that image, Michelle gave many speeches. The most widely watched was at the Democratic National Convention in August 2008. She talked about her marriage and children. She also stressed the Obamas' family values.

Unfair Treatment

Talking about her family and its values did not bother Michelle. She was not the first to do it. All the First Ladies before her said

PERSPECTIVES

CHILD CARE DURING THE CAMPAIGN

The Obamas had two young daughters. Michelle thought about who would care for the girls while she was busy making speeches. She asked her mother to help. Now she knew the children would be well cared for. It was vital to "keep their lives on track," she told an interviewer. "How do we keep our [family] traditions whole? Those are the day-to-day concerns."

similar things. What bothered her was that some people treated her differently than past potential First Ladies. She felt her race was the reason they did so.

Some people implied that she might not be a loyal American. One major magazine put a cartoon of her and her husband on its cover. It depicted them as terrorists. None of the white presidential candidates and their wives were portrayed that way, Michelle pointed out.

The pressure kept her awake at night. At first she worried about how people saw her. Were the lies hurting her husband's campaign, she wondered? Over time, however, she decided it was best to ignore the lies. This approach worked. Barack Obama won the election on November 4, 2008. The family celebrated the victory in front of thousands of supporters in Chicago. Michelle stood proudly at Obama's side.

STRAIGHT TO THE
SOURCE

In late August 2008, Michelle gave a speech at the Democratic National Convention. She said:

What struck me when I first met Barack was that even though he had this funny name, even though he'd grown up all the way across the continent in Hawaii, his family was so much like mine. He was raised by grandparents who were working-class folks just like my parents, and by a single mother who struggled to pay the bills just like we did. Like my family, they scrimped and saved so that he could have opportunities they never had themselves. And Barack and I were raised with so many of the same values: that you work hard for what you want in life; that your word is your bond and you do what you say you're going to do; that you treat people with dignity and respect, even if you don't know them, and even if you don't agree with them.

Source: "Transcript: Michelle Obama's Convention Speech." *NPR.* NPR, August 25, 2008. Web. Accessed October 3, 2017.

Back It Up

In this excerpt from the convention speech, Michelle uses evidence to support a point. Write a paragraph that identifies that point, and include two or three pieces of evidence that she uses to make it.

25

CHAPTER FOUR

AN INSPIRED CAMPAIGN MANAGER

One of the keys to Barack Obama's victory in 2008 was his skilled campaign manager. David Plouffe grew up in Wilmington, Delaware. He was born there on May 27, 1967. After high school, he attended the University of Delaware. There he gained an interest in politics. He left school in 1989 to pursue a political career.

It did not take long for the young man to find work. In 1990 he joined the campaign to reelect Iowa senator Tom Harkin. In the years that followed, Plouffe managed several other campaigns. Plouffe became well known

Along with running the campaign, David Plouffe occasionally gave speeches.

among Washington, DC, insiders. That was how Obama heard about him. After deciding to run for president, Obama needed capable advisers. So he hired Plouffe.

Organization and Money

Plouffe's first job as campaign manager was to find and organize a staff. It had to be very large. Presidential campaigns involve a huge number of tasks and duties. Some people handle operations. They make sure that campaign workers across the country are doing their jobs. Others schedule and manage upcoming rallies and other events. Still others handle the campaign's finances. Plouffe oversaw all these people. He kept track of the many campaign workers on a daily basis.

Another of Plouffe's main duties was to create a strategy to win the election. He and fellow Obama advisor David Axelrod came up with a plan. They needed to focus on several things. One was raising enough money. Campaign workers had to be paid.

Plouffe stayed busy. He spoke with reporters even while traveling.

LONG HOURS

Plouffe has done many interviews both during and after the campaign. In one, someone asked how many hours he put in each day. Plouffe responded that presidential campaigns are very time consuming. Those involved do nothing else. The only time people aren't usually working is between 1:00 a.m. and 5:00 a.m.

Television and radio ads are costly. So are planes and buses used to travel from state to state.

The question was how to raise the needed funds. Plouffe knew that most previous political campaigns relied on a few large donations. These typically came from a few wealthy individuals and groups. But he saw a better way to raise the money. He was sure that many ordinary Americans would contribute money to the campaign. Each donation might be small. But they would add up over time. There had to be a place people could go to donate. So Plouffe set up a website, and he was proven right. Millions of people sent money

Plouffe figured out which states Obama needed to sway in order to win. They focused the campaign on these states.

to the campaign. Obama raised more than $600 million over the Internet. That was 20 times as much as his opponent McCain raised.

Looking like a President

Another key strategy for winning involved public images. First there was Obama's image. Plouffe realized the importance of making him look like a president. Voters had to be comfortable picturing Obama as the nation's military commander. There was also his name—Barack Hussein Obama. Some Americans might have felt it sounded foreign. The campaign worked to depict him as an everyday American voters could relate to.

At the same time, the campaign needed to address McCain's image. Only it had to be negative rather than positive. Thus Plouffe and his staff worked hard to portray McCain as just another Washington politician.

PERSPECTIVES
GETTING INVOLVED

Plouffe had experience working in campaigns before managing one. He started as a volunteer going door-to-door to raise support for a candidate. He helped organize other volunteers. In an interview, Plouffe offered advice to others who want to work in campaigns:

Volunteer on a campaign, or work as staff on one, and see if you like it. If you do, keep working on them, which may require you to move around the country, and you will quickly gain more experience and responsibility. Elections matter in this country.

Plouffe was thrilled when Obama won the election. Afterward someone asked him if he needed to believe in a candidate's values in order to manage the campaign. Plouffe said, "Ideally, you work for someone who inspires you and shares many of your views on key issues and most importantly, know why they are running." That was a major reason for the victory. Plouffe shared Obama's vision for change.

FURTHER EVIDENCE

Chapter Four talks about Obama's campaign manager, David Plouffe, and how he ran the winning 2008 presidential campaign. What is one of the chapter's main points? What key evidence supports this point? Go to the article at the website below. Find a quote from the website that supports one of the chapter's main points.

UNIVERSITY OF DELAWARE: SEE HOW THEY RUN
abdocorelibrary.com/barack-obama-elected

CHAPTER FIVE

WAR HERO AND MAVERICK SENATOR

Barack Obama's opponent in the 2008 election was John McCain. McCain was born on August 29, 1936. His father, also named John McCain, was a naval officer. At the time, the elder McCain was stationed in Panama, where the younger McCain was born.

Young McCain's grandfather had also been a naval officer. There was a family tradition of serving in the US Navy. McCain wanted to

In 1961, McCain, *left*, and his parents stood as a navy training base was named for his grandfather, who was also in the navy.

follow that tradition. As a young man, he attended the Naval Academy at Annapolis, Maryland.

McCain later fought in the Vietnam War (1954–1975). He flew jets over North Vietnam. The enemy shot down his plane and captured him. He remained a prisoner from 1967 to 1973. His captors treated him brutally. When he was finally released, Americans saw him as a true war hero.

Independent Rebel

A few years after his return from the war, McCain settled in Arizona. In 1982 he decided to run for the US House of Representatives. He won and was reelected in 1984. Two years later, he ran for the US Senate and won.

McCain was a conservative Republican. But he did not always agree with other members of his party. So sometimes he voted with the Democrats. In this way, he earned a reputation as a maverick.

Clashes with Obama

McCain hoped his maverick image would help him become president. In April 2007, he entered the presidential race. During the campaign, he debated Obama several times on national TV. These clashes showed that the two men disagreed on many issues. One of their biggest differences was the ongoing Iraq War (2003–2011). Many Americans wanted the United States to leave Iraq.

The war was a hot topic in the first debate. McCain backed US involvement in the Iraq conflict. He said the United States was winning. It would not be defeated, he insisted.

MCCAIN'S FIRST PRESIDENTIAL BID

The 2008 race was not John McCain's first run for president. He also ran in the Republican primary election from 1999 to 2000. His main opponent was Texas governor George W. Bush. McCain traveled the country in a bus he called the "Straight Talk Express." But Bush collected far more support than McCain. The maverick senator had no choice but to withdraw.

PERSPECTIVES

DISAGREEMENT OVER THE ECONOMY

In the first presidential debate on September 26, 2008, McCain and Obama clashed over the US economy. Obama insisted that it was in poor shape. Major financial reforms were needed. Rich people were getting richer while ordinary workers were struggling to pay their bills. McCain countered that the economy was basically sound. Some reforms might be needed, he said. But any financial troubles were only temporary. "I have a fundamental belief in the goodness and strength of the American worker," McCain stated. "And I still believe, under the right leadership, our best days are ahead of us."

Obama disagreed. He questioned the wisdom of the war. More than 4,000 Americans had been killed. He thought it was time for a new policy in Iraq.

Why Obama Won

National polls showed that both critics and the public agreed that Obama had won all the debates. Most later polls predicted McCain would lose the election. When Obama won the election, political experts discussed why McCain had lost. First,

The first debate was held in Oxford, Mississippi.

they said, his position on the war hurt him. Two-thirds of Americans opposed the conflict. Another factor was money. Obama had hugely outspent McCain.

There was also the issue of McCain's running mate. He had chosen Sarah Palin, a former governor of Alaska. Many voters saw her as too inexperienced to be vice president.

McCain was gracious in defeat. By tradition, the losing candidate in an election concedes, or admits defeat. Usually he or she does so in a

US ELECTION MAP

This map shows which states Obama and McCain won in the 2008 election. One of Nebraska's five electoral votes went to Obama. Why do you think candidates had success in different states?

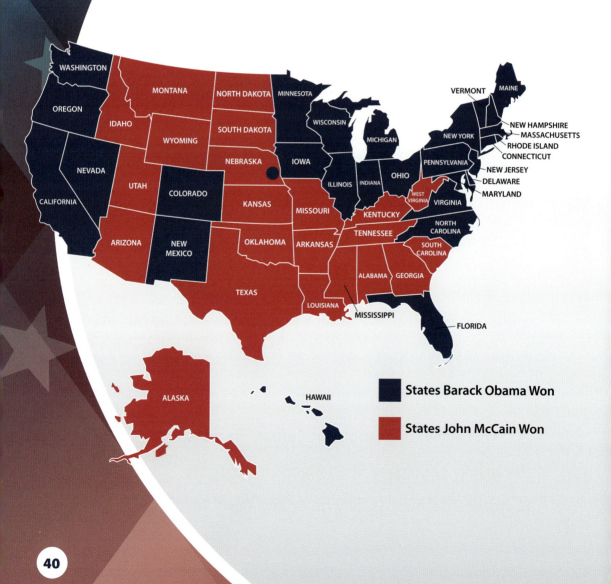

concession speech. When he lost to Obama, McCain pointed out that the American people had spoken quite clearly. He recalled how he had phoned Obama and congratulated him on his victory. McCain also said that he respected Obama's ability to inspire the hopes of many millions of Americans.

Although disappointed at losing the election, McCain had recognized an important reality. Obama had indeed inspired huge numbers of Americans. Some had voted for him because they felt that it was time to elect an African-American president. Others believed his policies would be good for the country. Still others admired him as a person. They saw him as intelligent, honorable, and eager to help ordinary people. Whatever their reasons for choosing Obama, voters had created a milestone in US politics. The American people had elected 43 white men in a row to the presidency. In 2008, they finally gave an African American a chance to serve in that lofty position.

IMPORTANT
DATES

1936
John McCain is born on August 29.

1961
Barack Obama is born on August 4.

1964
Michelle LaVaughn Robinson is born on January 17.

1967
David Plouffe is born on May 27.

1996
Obama is elected as an Illinois state senator.

2004
Obama is elected as a US senator.

2007
Obama formally announces he is running for president on February 10. John McCain enters the race in April.

2008
Obama delivers his famous "race speech" on March 18. Michelle gives a speech at the Democratic National Convention in August. On November 2, Obama is confident he will win the election. He wins the election on November 4.

STOP AND
THINK

Surprise Me

Chapter Three tells about Michelle Obama's background, how she met Barack Obama, and what she did to help on his presidential campaign. What two or three facts about Michelle and her experiences did you find most surprising? Write a few sentences about each fact and tell why you found it surprising.

Dig Deeper

After reading this book, what questions do you still have about Barack Obama's 2008 election? With an adult's help, find a few reliable sources that can help you answer your questions. Write a paragraph about what you learned.

Say What?

Studying the workings of a political campaign can mean learning a lot of new vocabulary. Find five words in this book you've never heard before. Use a dictionary to find out what they mean. Then write the meanings in your own words, and use each word in a new sentence.

GLOSSARY

candidate
someone who is running for public office

conservative
in politics, someone who is traditional and prefers to see change happen very gradually

electoral vote
a vote for a president cast by an elector, one of several people in each state who represent the entire state's vote

impoverished
poor

legislative bill
a suggested new law

maverick
someone who tends to be independent and not follow the majority

national convention
a large meeting held every four years to announce a party's presidential nominee

political science
the study of politics and governments

poll
a survey taken of a small group of people in an attempt to reflect the opinions of a larger group

primary
an election where voters select a party's candidate

ONLINE RESOURCES

To learn more about Barack Obama's 2008 election, visit our free resource websites below.

Visit **abdocorelibrary.com** for free Common Core resources for teachers and students, including vetted activities, multimedia, and booklinks, for deeper subject comprehension.

Visit **abdobooklinks.com** for free additional online weblinks for further learning. These links are routinely monitored and updated to provide the most current information available.

LEARN MORE

Cunningham, Kevin. *How Political Campaigns and Elections Work.* Minneapolis, MN: Abdo, 2015.

Stine, Megan. *Who Is Michelle Obama?* New York: Grosset and Dunlap, 2013.

ABOUT THE AUTHOR

Duchess Harris, JD, PhD
Professor Harris is the chair of the American Studies department at Macalester College and curator of the Duchess Harris Collection of ABDO books. She is the author and coauthor of recently released ABDO books including *Hidden Human Computers: The Black Women of NASA*, *Black Lives Matter*, and *Race and Policing*.

Before working with ABDO, she authored several other books on the topics of race, culture, and American history. She served as an associate editor for *Litigation News*, the American Bar Association Section of Litigation's quarterly flagship publication, and was the first editor in chief of *Law Raza*, an interactive online journal covering race and the law, published at William Mitchell College of Law. She has earned a PhD in American Studies from the University of Minnesota and a JD from William Mitchell College of Law.

INDEX

Black Panther Party, 15
Bush, George W., 37

campaign slogan, 16
campaign strategies, 28–32
children, 22–23
Columbia University, 14

debates, 37–38
Democratic National Convention, 16, 23, 25
Democratic Party, 5, 16
Democrats, 36
discrimination, 22
Dunham, Ann, 13

economy, 38
education, 13–14, 21
Electoral College, 10, 40

First Lady, 22, 23–24

Harkin, Tom, 27
Harvard University, 14, 21
Hawaii, 13, 25
Hendricks, Obery, 9
House of Representatives, US, 15, 36

Illinois state senate, 15
Iraq War, 37–38

marriage, 15, 21, 22, 23
McCain, John, 5, 9, 10, 31, 32, 35–41

Obama, Barack, Sr., 13
Obama, Michelle (née Robinson), 15, 21–24, 25

Palin, Sarah, 39
Plouffe, David, 27–33
presidential election, 9–10, 24, 28, 33, 35, 38–41
Princeton University, 21

race relations, 8, 9, 11
Republicans, 15, 36, 37
Rush, Bobby, 15

Senate, US, 15, 36
speeches, 5, 6–8, 9, 11, 16, 17, 23, 25, 41

Trinity Church, 6

University of Delaware, 27

Vietnam War, 36
volunteering, 32

Wills, Garry, 9
Wright, Jeremiah, 6–8, 9